Haaland

The Complete Story of a Football Superstar

100+ Interesting Trivia Questions, Interactive Activities, and Random, Shocking Fun Facts Every Fan Needs to Know

HOUSE OF BALLERS

YOUR FREE BONUS!

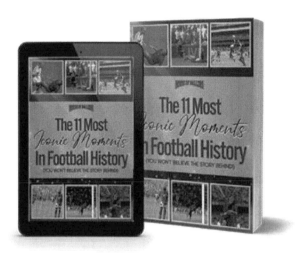

>> SCAN THE QR CODE BELOW TO GAIN EXCLUSIVE ACCESS <<

The 11 Most Iconic Moments in Football History

In this special edition, you'll discover the secret stories behind them.

Enjoy!

Contents

INTRODUCTION

Nobody knows what Erling Haaland is!

A robot? A Nordic monster that feeds off his opponents' fears and weaknesses? A genetically-modified superhuman? A computer program functioning with brutal efficiency?

Your guess is as good as mine. But what is sure is that the Norwegian super-striker, Erling Haaland, is from out of this world. Incredibly agile; blessed with blistering pace and raw strength; able to finish chances with aplomb; he strikes terror into the minds of all defenses that come up against him. And he is still only 22!

Erling Haaland first came into the limelight by scoring a competition-record 9 goals for Norway against Honduras at the 2019 FIFA Under-20 World Cup in Poland. Since then, the 6'4" tall striker has morphed into one of the finest players in his position, plundering in lots of goals and setting numerous records along the way.

Haaland is gifted with a towering frame which he uses to hold up play, clever movement to make excellent runs behind opposition defenses, and excellent finishing technique that has made him arguably the most fearsome striker on the planet.

After his father's injury-ending career that eventually led to the family's return to Norway, Haaland embraced his destiny as the person to inherit his father's status as a professional footballer. He rose rapidly through the youth ranks at Bryn FK and was soon playing at Molde FK under Manchester United legend Ole Gunnar Solskjaer.

But it was at Red Bull Salzburg where he truly made his name as a prolific marksman. On the back of his exploits at the 2019 FIFA Under-20 World Cup, Haaland scored in each of his club's opening five UEFA Champions League group stage games, including a hattrick on his debut in the competition. He secured a move to Borussia Dortmund at the start of 2020 and scored 86 goals in 89 appearances before moving to Manchester City, the club where his father's career effectively ended.

Today, Haaland is arguably the first person any football enthusiast thinks about when the topic of scoring goals at a consistent rate is brought up. In his first season in English football, he has already eclipsed most of the illustrious names who have played in the Premier League before him. In fact, he is set to break the all-time record for Premier League goals in a single season in his debut season.

But what is his story? How did his father's injury change the course of his destiny? What are the secrets behind his elite performances?

This book answers these and many other questions about the heir to Ronaldo and Messi's goal-scoring throne. In ten chapters, this book tells the story of Erling Braut Haaland. From his childhood in Bryne, his love for meditation, and his iconic celebrations, every inch of Haaland's life has been tailored towards the creation of the phenomenal goal-scoring machine that he is now!

Sit back, relax, and have fun reading about Erling Haaland, the Nordic monster who cannot stop scoring!

CHAPTER

1

BIRTH & CHILDHOOD

"I was born in England. I have been a City fan my whole life. I know a lot about the club."

– Erling Haaland.

Erling Braut Haaland was born on 21 July 2000 in Leeds, West Yorkshire, England. At the time of his birth, his father, Alfie Haaland, was a player at Leeds United Football Club. His mother's name was Gry Marita Braut, and she had two children before Erling; Astor, his brother, and Gabrielle, his sister. Gry Marita Braut was a former heptathlete, a competition in which each athlete competes in seven different track and field events.

After starting his career at Bryne FK, Alfie Haaland spent ten years in England playing for Nottingham Forest, Leeds United, and Manchester City. Erling enjoyed a harmonious relationship with his siblings while growing up as he smiled a lot and was full of energy. He has his ancestral roots in Bryne, a small town in Rogaland County, Norway.

In 2004, Haaland's family left England for their hometown of Bryne following an injury to his father, which effectively ended his playing career. Haaland was brought up in Bryne, where most of the 12,000 inhabitants at the time were passionate about football.

In 2006, Haaland was enrolled at Bryne Footballklubb, a sports institution that suited his yearnings. He received good sports education and participated in a raft of other sports, like handball, golf, and heptathlon, besides football. He even broke a world record in the long jump, winning the award for his age category at the time for the highest-standing long jump (1.63 m) in 2006.

Haaland had health issues relating to stunted growth in his teenage years while at Molde FK, impacting his performance on the football pitch. Fortunately, Molde had seasoned people on their staff, such as fitness coach Borre Steenslid and chef, Torbjerg "Tanta" Haugen, amongst others, who helped Haaland overcome his health issues and forge ahead in his journey to becoming one of the world's best footballers.

10 Trivia Questions

1. Where was Erling Haaland born?

    A. Oslo, Norway

    B. Leeds, United Kingdom

    C. Jacksonville, Florida

    D. Manchester, United Kingdom

2. When was Erling Haaland born?

    A. July 21, 2000.

    B. April 1, 2004.

    C. July 21, 1999.

    D. February 12, 2002.

3. What is Haaland's full name?

    A. Erling Oscar Haaland

    B. Erling Jacob Haaland

    C. Erling Braut Haaland

    D. Erling Erik Braut Haaland

4. How old was Haaland when his family moved back to Norway?

    A. 9

    B. 3

    C. 10

    D. 13

5. What is the name of Haaland's father?

   A. Erling Haaland Sr.

   B. Elias Haaland

   C. Alfie Haaland

   D. John Carew

6. How old was Haaland when he was enrolled at Bryne FK?

   A. 7

   B. 5

   C. 5

   D. 4

7. In what sport did Haaland set a world record as a kid?

   A. Javelin

   B. Boxing

   C. Karate

   D. Long jump

8. What is the name of Haaland's mother?

   A. Maria Braut

   B. Gry Maria Braut

   C. Gry Marita Braut

   D. Marina Braut

9. Where was Erling Haaland brought up?

   A. Bryne

   B. Leeds

   C. Oslo

   D. Nottingham

10. When did Haaland's family leave the United Kingdom?

    A. 2001

    B. 2002

    C. 2003

    D. 2004

10 Trivia Answers

1. B – Leeds, United Kingdom

2. A – July 21, 2000

3. C – Erling Braut Haaland

4. B – 3

5. C – Alfie Haaland

6. B – 5

7. D – Long jump

8. C – Gry Marita Braut

9. A – Bryne

10. D – 2004

ERLING HAALAND MAZE #1

GOAL

CHAPTER

2

FORAY INTO FOOTBALL & YOUTH CAREER

"I saw Erling for the first time when he joined our indoor training. Haaland's first two touches led to goals. Because he was so much better than the others, we immediately pulled him up to play with boys a year older than him."

– Alf Ingve Bernstein.

Haaland had very good sports genes, as both of his parents were active athletes. He grew up in a household that lived and breathed sports to become a confident, lively, and energetic kid who played football with his friends and siblings from an early age. He decided to focus only on football from the age of six after he was enrolled at Bryne FK, an indoor sports academy in his hometown where his father also began his football career.

Haaland rose quickly through the youth ranks at FC Bryne and developed into a good player with unequaled football ability among his peers and was terrific in front of goal. Smiling a lot, training a lot, and scoring lots of goals are traits from his childhood he has retained to this day. He was known for his shooting and finishing skills throughout his stay at FK Bryne, a reputation that earned him a call-up to Norway's national youth team, whom he helped win the Syrenka Cup.

Haaland's meteoric rise through the youth ranks at Bryne FK continued as he scored 18 goals in 14 matches for Bryne FK's reserve team. He made his debut for the first team in May 2016, shortly before his 16th birthday, following the appointment of Bryne's youth coach Alf Ingve Bernstein as caretaker boss. Bernstein moved Haaland to his preferred role as a striker after he had initially been deployed as a winger.

Haaland's 16 appearances for Bryne's senior team were enough to attract interest from clubs at home and abroad, first receiving an offer of a trial from German outfit 1899 Hoffenheim, which his parents swiftly rejected. His eye-catching performances shot him to the top of Molde FK's transfer wish list, and a deal was soon struck between Bryne FK and Molde FK for Haaland's transfer to the latter club, who was managed by Ole Gunnar Solskjaer. Molde revealed the capture of 16-year-old Haaland on 1st February 2017.

10 Trivia Questions

1. How old was Haaland when he joined his hometown club's academy?

    A. 5

    B. 6

    C. 7

    D. 4

2. How many goals did Haaland score for Bryne Reserves in 14 matches?

    A. 18

    B. 6

    C. 21

    D. 14

3. In which season did Haaland make a senior debut for Bryne?

    A. 2015/16

    B. 2016/17

    C. 2014/15

    D. 2018/19

4. Which role was Haaland initially deployed in while at Bryne FK?

    A. Central defender

    B. Centre-forward

    C. Midfielder

    D. Winger

5. How many senior appearances did Haaland make for Bryne FK?

    A. 19

    B. 24

    C. 12

    D. 16

6. How many goals did Haaland score for Bryne FK's first team?

    A. 0

    B. 2

    C. 5

    D. 7

7. What is the name of the Bryne coach that handed Haaland his senior debut?

    A. Torbjerg Haugen

    B. Borre Steenslid

    C. Alf Ingve Bernsten

    D. Ole Gunnar Solsjkaer

8. Which German club offered Haaland a trial while he was at Bryne?

    A. 1860 Munich

    B. 1899 Hoffenheim

    C. Hannover 96

    D. Hamburger SV

9. How old was Haaland when he joined Molde FK?

    A. 14

    B. 19

    C. 17

    D. 16

10. When did Molde announce the signing of Haaland?

    A. 1 February 2017

    B. 1 January 2017

    C. 31 December 2016

    D. 31 January 2017

10 Trivia Answers

1. A – 5

2. A – 18

3. B – 2016/17

4. D – Winger

5. D – 16

6. A – 0

7. C – Alf Ingve Bernsten

8. B – 1899 Hoffenheim

9. D – 16

10. A – 1 February 2017

ERLING HAALAND WORD SEARCH #1

```
M  L  B  E  R  L  I  N  G  M  R  B  D  H  B
P  T  H  H  A  A  L  A  N  D  F  K  D  U  P
B  M  D  Q  N  K  C  U  S  G  R  V  Y  C  A
I  B  Y  J  T  O  P  S  C  O  R  E  R  H  J
U  L  I  D  D  O  R  T  M  U  N  D  X  F  D
S  A  L  Z  B  U  R  G  H  N  B  G  G  C  W
E  N  G  L  A  N  D  B  C  O  U  Z  E  A  I
D  I  R  A  Z  N  S  R  W  R  N  E  R  Y  W
Z  H  C  H  U  J  I  D  H  W  D  S  M  D  L
Y  X  I  C  K  K  R  E  Q  A  E  P  A  M  Q
F  B  T  N  O  Y  M  J  O  Y  S  H  N  T  K
A  J  Y  Q  N  K  Z  B  C  S  L  M  Y  O  D
X  U  Z  C  Y  E  P  L  C  X  I  N  U  Z  X
Q  H  E  M  A  N  C  I  T  Y  G  M  Z  S  Y
E  Y  N  D  R  U  F  V  L  O  A  Z  E  Q  X
```

ERLING	EPL	DORTMUND	ENGLAND
NORWAY	BUNDESLIGA	GERMANY	MANCITY
CITYZEN	SALZBURG	HAALAND	TOPSCORER

CHAPTER

3

BREAKTHROUGH AT MOLDE & MOVE TO RB SALZBURG

"That's my alarm tone (Champions League theme song). I wake up to it every day. It's the last song I'd get tired of. I wake up to it, so I always get a perfect start to the day."

– Erling Haaland.

Haaland made his debut for Molde on 26th April 2017 in a Norwegian Cup game against Volda Tl and scored a goal to help his side win 3-2. He made his league debut against Sarpsborg 08 on 4 June, coming on as a substitute and immediately picking up a booking before he scored the winner soon after. He netted another crucial goal in a 3-2 win over FK Viking on 17th September and finished his first season at the club with 4 goals in 20 appearances.

Haaland scored four times in the opening quarter of the game to help Molde beat unbeaten league leaders Brann, 4-0 on July 1st, 2018, leading then Molde manager Ole Gunnar Solskjaer to compare Haaland's style to that of Belgian striker Romelu Lukaku. Solskjaer also disclosed that the club had turned down several offers for their highly-rated forward.

Haaland extended his remarkable form in front of goal with a brace a week later in a 5-1 win over Valeranga and scored his first goal in UEFA Competition when Molde beat KF Laci in a Europa League qualifying round match. Haaland missed Molde's final 3 games of the season due to a sprained ankle but still received the 2018 Eliteserien Breakthrough of the Year award after finishing as Molde's highest goalscorer of the 2018 season with 16 goals in 30 games across all competitions.

On August 19th,2018, Austrian Bundesliga club Red Bull Salzburg disclosed that Haaland would join the club on January 1st, 2019, after a deal was agreed upon with Molde FK for his transfer. A reporter from an English tabloid also revealed that Haaland had been the subject of a failed bid from Leeds United, one of the clubs his father featured for during his playing days.

Haaland made his debut for RB Salzburg in an Austrian Cup game against Wiener Neustadter, played on February 17th, 2019. His first goal for the club came in a 2-1 win over LASK in an Austrian Bundesliga game played on May 12. He scored a first hattrick for the club on 19th July, in a 7-1 rout of SC-ESV Parndorf in the Austrian Cup. He scored further hattricks against Wolfsberger AC in the Austrian Bundesliga and against Genk in his first UEFA Champions League game for RB Salzburg. He scored in each of his side's next four Champions League games to become the first teenager to score in the first 5 successive Champions League appearances and the sixth player to score in the first 5 games of a Champions League group stage. He did not find the target in the final group game against Liverpool, eventually his last appearance for the club. He left the club having scored a total of 29 goals, with 28 of those scored in just 22 appearances made during the 2019/20 campaign.

10 Trivia Questions

1. When did Haaland join Molde?

   A. 2011

   B. 2016

   C. 2014

   D. 2017

2. When did Haaland make his debut for Molde?

   A. April 2017

   B. February 2017

   C. December 2018

   D. August 2017

3. Against which club did Haaland score a hattrick on his Champions League debut with RB Salzburg?

   A. Liverpool

   B. Dortmund

   C. Genk

   D. Napoli

4. How many goals did Haaland score during the 2019/20 season at RB Salzburg?

   A. 10

   B. 48

   C. 28

   D. 11

5. What was the duration of Haaland's contract with RB Salzburg?

   A. 5 years

   B. 2 years

   C. 3 years

   D. 6 years

6. How many goals did Haaland score in his first season with Molde?

   A. 15

   B. 7

   C. 2

   D. 4

7. Against which team did Haaland score his first goal in a UEFA competition?

   A. Valeranga

   B. KF Laci

   C. Sarpsborg

   D. Volda Tl

8. How many goals did Haaland score for Molde in the 2018 season?

   A. 39

   B. 10

   C. 16

   D. 25

9. When did RB Salzburg announce the signing of Haaland?

   A. August 2018

   B. January August 2018

   C. December 2018

   D. January 2019

10. Against which team did Haaland make his RB Salzburg debut?

    A. LASK

    B. Parndorf

    C. Wolfsberger

    D. Weiner Neustadter

10 Trivia Answers

1. D – 2017

2. A – 26 April 2017

3. C – Genk

4. C – 28

5. A – 5 years

6. D – 4

7. B – KF Laci

8. C – 16

9. A – 19 August 2018

10. D- Weiner Neustadter

ERLING HAALAND WORD SCRAMBLE #1

1. HCMERESTAN TYIC _____

2. SIOSURAB UOTDDNRM _____

3. GRLINE AALNHDA _____

4. WRONAY _____

5. ELEDS _____

6. EBAUSLINGD _____

7. BR GLRSBZUA _____

8. LNHISEG RPIMERE UELGEA _____

9. ERNGMAY _____

10. EPP AUIODRALG _____

11. NVKIE ED REUNYB _____

12. AKIYI DGGUNAON _____

13. NREBMU ENIN _____

14. SOHNDMEA _____

15. RTESKRI _____

16. LAGO RSCOER _____

17. CDROER BKEARRE _____

18. FYTEL _____

19. CMAOR SREU _____

20. DEJU IGENHLMLAB _____

CHAPTER

4
INTERNATIONAL CAREER

"And for Norway, it's brilliant we have a striker who can score goals again."

– Ole Gunnar Solskjaer

Haaland represented Norway at various youth levels before he started playing for the senior side. He scored a hattrick for Norway under-18 in a 5-4 win over Scotland in March 2018 to help them secure a place in the 2018 UEFA European under-19 Championship.

At the tournament proper, Haaland scored a penalty in a 1-1 draw with Italy and scored 9 goals in Norway's 12-0 rout of Honduras at the 2019 FIFA under-20 World Cup in Lublin, Poland. With that, he set a competition record for most goals scored by a player in a single match and finished as the competition's top scorer despite netting no further goals in Norway's other two fixtures as they exited the competition in the group stage.

In August 2019, Haaland was included in Norway's squad for UEFA Euro 2020 qualifiers against Sweden and Malta, and he made his senior international debut on 5th September 2019 against Malta. His first senior international goal came in a 1-2 loss to Austria in September 2020. However, he netted a brace in a 5-1 win over Northern Ireland three days later. Haaland made it 6 goals in 6 senior international games with a hattrick in a 4-0 win over Romania in October 2020. In the three 2022 World Cup qualification matches played in September 2021, Haaland scored 5 goals, including a second international hattrick in Norway's 5-1 rout of Gibraltar.

10 Trivia Questions

1. At which international youth level did Haaland score a hat-trick against Scotland in 2018?

    A. Under-16

    B. Under-19

    C. Under-20

    D. Under-23

2. Against which team did Haaland score 9 goals in a single international match?

    A. Panama

    B. Haiti

    C. Honduras

    D. Jamaica

3. At which tournament did Haaland score 9 goals in a single match?

    A. 2018 under-19 Euros

    B. 2017 FIFA under-17 World Cup

    C. 2019 FIFA under-17 World Cup

    D. 2019 FIFA under-20 World Cup

4. When did Haaland win the Syrenka Cup with Norway under-17?

   A. 2016

   B. 2014

   C. 2015

   D. 2018

5. How many matches did Haaland play for Norway at the 2019 FIFA under-20 World Cup?

   A. 0

   B. 3

   C. 1

   D. 2

6. When did Haaland make his senior debut for Norway?

   A. September 2019

   B. December 2019

   C. March 2019

   D. August 2019

7. Which team did Haaland score his first senior goal for Norway against?

   A. Sweden

   B. Malta

   C. Austria

   D. Northern Ireland

8. Which team did Haaland score his first senior international hat-trick against?

   A. Romania

   B. Northern Ireland

   C. Gibraltar

   D. Netherlands

9. How many senior appearances has Haaland made for Norway (as of February 2023)?

    A. 30

    B. 12

    C. 23

    D. 44

10. How many goals has Haaland scored for Norway's senior national team (as of February 2023)?

    A. 24

    B. 23

    C. 22

    D. 21

10 Trivia Answers

1. **B – Under-19**

2. **C – Honduras**

3. **D – 2019 FIFA under-20 World Cup**

4. **A – 2016**

5. **B – 3**

6. **A – September 2019**

7. **C – Austria**

8. **A – Romania**

9. **C -23**

10. **D – 21**

ERLING HAALAND WORD SEARCH #2

```
T G P B A E G I M I F H G Z G
Z H U N B C H E I G H T U Y H
G O A L S C O R E R N H A V A
P A M R E C O R D J J M R L N
A J E Q B B K T M F G A D S D
C M W S X U O V M A R N I D S
E N U M B E R N I N E C O B O
Z U B W P L P S S G A H L B M
B G X D U E O P D H A E A T E
J V L K G F W E S A W S K C P
U E Y O A T E E U R R T W C A
V Q Z U A Y R D V Q J E V F F
Y F S T R I K E R J T R J R B
Z S K B P E Y H N F S A E M X
N W S W S K M D W F A S E H J
```

HANDSOME	GOALSCORER	GUARDIOLA	HEIGHT
NUMBERNINE	RECORD	SPEED	MANCHESTER
PACE	STRIKER	POWER	LEFTY

CHAPTER

5

CAREER ACHIEVEMENTS

"I am so upset with him (Haaland). He didn't score three goals, so that's why the petition to sack him from the Premier League isn't going to happen."

– Pep Guardiola

Despite being only 22, Erling Haaland has racked up a respectable number of achievements in his promising career. He helped Norway's under-17 win the Syrenka Cup in 2016, won the Golden Boot at the FIFA under-20 World Cup in 2019, and was awarded the coveted Golden Boy prize for the best young male footballer in Europe in 2020.

Back in Norway, Haaland was named Eliteserien Breakthrough of the Year in 2018 and Norwegian Sportsperson of the Year in 2020. He also won the Kniksen's honor award in 2020 and the Gullballen in 2020 and 2021.

Haaland has won the Austrian Bundesliga twice, the Austrian Cup once, and the DFB Pokal once. He finished as the top goalscorer in the 2020/21 UEFA Champions League and was named UEFA Champions League 2020/21 Forward of the Season. He also finished as the top goalscorer in the 2020/21 UEFA Nations League and was named in the 2021 FIFA FIFPro World XI.

Haaland was named Austrian Footballer of the Year in 2019 and Austrian Bundesliga Player of the 2019/20 season. He made the UEFA Champions League Breakthrough XI in 2019 and was named Bundesliga Player of the Season in 2020/21. He has been named in the Bundesliga Team of the Season on two occasions and in the ESM Team of the Year for 2019/20. Haaland has won Bundesliga Player of the Month four times, Bundesliga Rookie of the Month twice, and the Bundesliga Goal of the Month in September 2021

Haaland won the first Premier League Player of the Month award given out in his first season at Manchester City, and has also been named as the PFA Premier League Fans' Player of the Month for August, September, and December, in 2022.

10 Trivia Questions

1. How many times did Haaland win the Austrian Bundesliga?

    A. Never

    B. Twice

    C. Thrice

    D. Four times

2. When did Haaland win the Golden Boy award?

    A. 2019

    B. 2018

    C. 2020

    D. 2021

3. When was Haaland named Norwegian Sportsperson of the Year?

    A. 2020

    B. 2019

    C. 2021

    D. 2018

4. On how many occasions did Haaland win the Bundesliga Player of the Month award?

    A. 3

    B. 4

    C. 5

    D. 2

5. In which season did Haaland win the Bundesliga Player of the Season award?

    A. 2019/20

    B. 2018/19

    C. 2021/22

    D. 2020/21

6. When was Haaland named Eliteserien Breakthrough of the Year?

    A. 2016

    B. 2017

    C. 2018

    D. 2019

7. How many major trophies did Haaland win with RB Salzburg?

    A. 5

    B. 3

    C. 0

    D. 1

8. Which trophy did Haaland win with Borussia Dortmund?

    A. DFB Pokal

    B. DFL-Super Cup

    C. Bundesliga

    D. UEFA Champions League

9. In which season did Haaland finish as the top goalscorer in the UEFA Champions League?

    A. 2018/19

    B. 2019/20

    C. 2020/21

    D. 2021/22

10. How many goals did Haaland score to win the Golden Boot at the 2019 FIFA under-20 World Cup?

    A. 12

    B. 11

    C. 10

    D. 9

10 Trivia Answers

1. B – Twice

2. C – 2020

3. A – 2020

4. B – 4

5. D – 2020/21

6. C – 2018

7. B – 3

8. A – DFB Pokal

9. C – 2020/21

10. D – 9

ERLING HAALAND MAZE #2

GOAL

CHAPTER

6
INDIVIDUAL RECORDS

"He's (Haaland) a machine. He's got the goal in his sights. He's destroyed us. He's only 19, and he's already a great No. 9. Imagine how far he could go."

– Jorge Mere

Since the time he lit up the group stage of the 2019/20 UEFA Champions League, Erling Haaland has set quite a number of astonishing individual records at RB Salzburg, Borussia Dortmund, and Manchester City. In only his first season at Manchester City, he has scored more Premier League hattricks (four) than any Manchester City player in a single Premier League season. He is the first player to score in his first four away Premier League games and also the fastest to reach 10, 15, 20, and 25 Premier League goals. He has broken Sergio Aguero's record for most Premier League goals in a season for Manchester City, with his 27th league goal of the campaign against Bournemouth in February 2023.

Haaland is the first teenager to score in his first 5 UEFA Champions League games, the sixth to score in the first 5 games of the UEFA Champions League group stage, and the quickest to reach 10, 15, and 20 UEFA Champions League goals. He has netted 28 times in just 22 UEFA Champions League games, bettering Harry Kane's previous record of 18 goals in 22 games. At 22 years and 47 days old, Haaland also became the youngest player to reach 25 Champions League goals.

Haaland is the only player to score more than once on his UEFA Champions League debut for three different teams. He netted a hattrick in his first-ever Champions League game for RB Salzburg against Genk, a brace in his Champions League debut for Borussia Dortmund against PSG, and another brace in his Champions League debut for Manchester City against Sevilla.

10 Trivia Questions

1. How old was Haaland when he became the youngest player to score 25 Champions League goals?

    A. 19 years old

    B. 22 years old

    C. 23 years old

    D. 20 years old

2. How many games did it take Haaland to reach 50 Bundesliga goals?

    A. 50 games

    B. 30 games

    C. 55 games

    D. 40 games

3. For how many clubs has Haaland scored multiple goals on his Champions League debut?

    A. 2

    B. 3

    C. 4

    D. 5

4. How many goals did Haaland score in his first 8 Premier League games?

   A. 8

   B. 10

   C. 12

   D. 14

5. How many players apart from Haaland have scored in the first 5 games of a Champions League group stage campaign?

   A. 2

   B. 0

   C. 5

   D. 1

6. How many Premier League hattricks has Haaland scored (as of February 2023)?

   A. 4

   B. 3

   C. 2

   D. 1

7. How many players apart from Haaland have scored in their first 4 Premier League away games?

   A. 0

   B. 1

   C. 2

   D. 3

8. Which team did Haaland score his second Premier League hattrick against?

   A. Wolves

   B. Crystal Palace

   C. Manchester United

   D. Nottingham Forest

9. Apart from Haaland, which other Dortmund player scored a hattrick on his Bundesliga debut?

    A.   Paco Alcacer

    B.   Marco Reus

    C.   Robert Lewandowski

    D.   Pierre-Emerick Aubameyang

10. How many goals did Haaland score in his first 3 Bundesliga games for Dortmund?

    A.   9

    B.   8

    C.   7

    D.   6

10 Trivia Answers

1. B – 22 years old

2. A – 50 games

3. B – 3

4. D – 14

5. C – 5

6. A – 4

7. A – 0

8. B – Crystal Palace

9. D – Pierre-Emerick Aubameyang

10. C – 7

ERLING HAALAND WORD SEARCH #3

```
F  K  B  O  B  E  L  L  I  N  G  H  A  M  D
D  F  S  H  W  B  T  I  V  Y  M  R  S  Y  P
P  M  T  X  U  Q  R  R  W  K  T  B  Y  C  L
Y  E  L  L  O  W  D  L  V  T  E  E  D  P  Y
L  F  D  E  B  R  U  Y  N  E  J  W  U  S  K
B  V  P  G  U  N  D  O  G  A  N  J  V  R  B
Z  H  I  C  L  E  Z  B  S  A  N  C  H  O  A
M  O  L  D  E  T  S  R  Q  Q  G  T  B  N  S
D  Y  E  M  D  F  S  Y  Y  S  Y  W  B  Q  U
Z  I  K  A  B  R  J  N  G  O  N  C  J  O  E
U  M  M  H  L  B  S  E  A  F  R  E  U  S  S
Q  C  Q  R  E  H  V  F  G  W  A  L  K  E  R
B  A  J  E  E  X  O  K  J  D  E  F  H  M  Z
K  I  X  Z  D  L  I  G  H  T  B  L  U  E  M
X  X  B  D  S  E  B  P  K  I  A  H  H  R  S
```

GUNDOGAN	BRYNEFK	MOLDE	YELLOW
MAHREZ	BELLINGHAM	LIGHTBLUE	WALKER
SANCHO	DEBRUYNE	REUS	LEEDS

CHAPTER

7

ICONIC MOMENTS

"Shout so early – he (Haaland) could be the greatest ever player in the Premier League. I've never seen a player so young have the desire to score the goals he scores. He's just relentless."

– John Terry

Haaland's promising career has been filled with some iconic moments. He first burst onto the scene with a competition record of 9 goals in Norway's 12-0 rout of Honduras at the 2019 FIFA under-20 World Cup, followed closely by goals in each of his first 5 UEFA Champions League games that included a hattrick for RB Salzburg against Genk.

Following his move to Borussia Dortmund in January 2020, Haaland continued his fine form in front of goal with a 23-minute hattrick on his Bundesliga debut as a substitute against Augsburg and a brace in the German side's 2-1 win over PSG in the 2019/20 UEFA Champions League Round of 16 first match leg to bring his tally of Champions League goals to 10 in his debut season in the competition.

Haaland scored the opening goal of Dortmund's 4-0 Revierderby wins over Schalke 04 in the first Bundesliga game after the break caused by the COVID-19 pandemic. Haaland finished the 2019/20 season with 44 goals in 40 club appearances across all competitions for both RB Salzburg and Borussia Dortmund. He scored the 100th goal of his senior career in a 4-2 loss at Bayern Munich in March 2021 and a brace in Dortmund's 4-1 win over RB Leipzig in 2020/21 DFB Pokal final. In his final appearance for Borussia Dortmund in May 2022, Haaland scored the opening goal of a 2-1 home win over Hertha Berlin.

Haaland scored a brace in his competitive debut for Manchester City, a 2-0 Premier League win at West Ham United. His first hattrick came in only his fourth league appearance, scoring three times in a 4-2 win over Crystal Palace. He scored another hattrick four days later, in a 6-0 win over Nottingham Forest, and a third Premier League hattrick in his first Manchester derby on October 2, becoming the first player to score hattricks in three straight home Premier League games.

10 Trivia Questions

1. For which team did Haaland score a hat trick in 14 minutes?

   A. RB Salzburg

   B. Manchester City

   C. Molde

   D. Borussia Dortmund

2. In which famous Bundesliga derby did Haaland score the infamous scissor-kick volley?

   A. Schalke 04 vs Borussia Dortmund

   B. Bayern Munich vs Borussia Dortmund

   C. Hamburger SV vs Borussia Dortmund

   D. Borussia Dortmund vs VfB Stuttgart

3. How many goals did Haaland score in his first Manchester derby?

   A. 1 goal

   B. 3 goals

   C. 4 goals

   D. 5 goals

4. Against which team did Haaland score the 100th goal of his senior career?

   A. Sevilla

   B. PSG

   C. Bayern Munich

   D. RB Leipzig

5. How many goals did Haaland score in his first season in the Champions League?

   A. 4

   B. 8

   C. 6

   D. 10

6. Against which team did Haaland play his final game for Borussia Dortmund?

   A. Hertha Berlin

   B. Union Berlin

   C. Koln

   D. Freiburg

7. Apart from Haaland, how many players have scored Premier League hattricks in three straight home games?

   A. 3

   B. 0

   C. 2

   D. 5

8. How many goals did Haaland score in Norway's win over Honduras at the 2019 FIFA under-20 World Cup?

   A. 6

   B. 7

   C. 8

   D. 9

9. Against which team did Haaland make his Premier League debut?

    A. Liverpool

    B. Aston Villa

    C. West Ham

    D. Bournemouth

10. In which month did Haaland win his first Premier League Player of the Month award?

    A. August

    B. September

    C. October

    D. December

10 Trivia Answers

1. D – Borussia Dortmund

2. A – Schalke 04 vs. Borussia Dortmund

3. B – 3 goals

4. C – Bayern Munich

5. D – 10

6. A – Hertha Berlin

7. B – 0

8. D – 9

9. C – West Ham

10. A – August

ERLING HAALAND WORD SCRAMBLE #2

1. ELINRG _____

2. AHADNLA _____

3. YAONWR _____

4. EYBNR KF _____

5. MEDLO KF _____

6. ERD LLBU ZBLSUAGR _____

7. BIUSSOAR MDDRUNOT _____

8. SEMCARNTEH ICYT _____

9. DEINSBAGLU _____

10. INEHSLG MREEPIR EUAGEL _____

CHAPTER

8

PERSONAL LIFE & PHILANTHROPY

"I sleep with five balls that I scored a hat trick with…I look at them every day. They are my girlfriends."

– Erling Haaland

According to Stanislav Macek, Haaland had a girlfriend during his time at Molde FK, but her studies prevented her from relocating with Haaland when the Norwegian forward transferred to RB Salzburg. The relationship ended in the final quarter of 2018. Haaland once told a reporter that he had five secret girlfriends, but he later clarified that the "five girlfriends" the matchday balls he received for scoring hattricks.

Haaland has maintained a harmonious relationship with members of his immediate family since childhood. His father, who he regards as a friend and mentor, was his personal trainer from the ages of 6 to 15 and still offers him advice on how to sustain excellence in his profession. His mother, Gry Marita, ensured Haaland and his siblings were brought up well and got all they needed to succeed. His older brother Astor is 1 cm taller and loves water and fish, while his older sister Gabrielle is believed to be in the Norwegian military and married to Jan Gunnar Elder, with whom she has two daughters. Haaland has a maternal cousin named Albert Braut Tjaaland, who is 19 years old and also a professional footballer.

Haaland's hobbies include chopping wood with a chainsaw, as splitting stacks of trees serves as a form of workout to help build his arms as well as a good exercise for his heart. He also likes meditation and potato farming, which he does during the summer break, which happens at the same time as the Norwegian frost-free planting season. Haaland has no tattoos and dislikes interviews, a trait he picked up from childhood as he despised being asked what he wants for dinner.

Apart from being one of the most lethal finishers in world football, Erling Haaland also does his bit for charity. He donated his autographed shirt worn in Dortmund's 4-0 Revierderby win over Schalke 04 to be auctioned, and the entire proceeds are given to Kinderlachen eV, an aid organization for children in Germany, Austria, and Switzerland.

At the end of Borussia Dortmund's UEFA Champions League quarterfinal meeting in April 2021, Romanian referee Octavian Sovre approached Haaland for an autograph on his yellow and red cards. The cards would later be auctioned and sold to raise funds for SOS Autism Bihor, a Romanian charitable effort providing support to people suffering from Autism.

During his enforced break as a result of Norway's non-participation at the 2022 World Cup in Qatar, Haaland took part in a charity exhibition match against Vivil IL, a team from Oslo that supports people with Down's Syndrome.

10 Trivia Questions

1. How many goals did Haaland score in the 2022 charity game held in Oslo?

   A. 5

   B. 10

   C. 15

   D. 20

2. Which charity benefited from the proceeds of a referee's red and yellow cards signed by Haaland?

   A. SOS Autism Bihor

   B. UNICEF

   C. Save the Children

   D. Kinderlachen eV

3. Against which team did Haaland refuse to celebrate a goal?

   A. RB Leipzig

   B. PSG

   C. Borussia Dortmund

   D. Bayern Munich

4. Who swapped jerseys with Haaland after Dortmund played Leverkusen in 2021?

    A. Gio Reyna

    B. Leverkusen coach

    C. A referee

    D. A Leverkusen player

5. For which of his previous club's teammates did Haaland spend £500K on farewell gifts?

    A. Bryne

    B. Molde

    C. RB Salzburg

    D. Borussia Dortmund

6. Which charity benefited from the proceeds of Haaland's auctioned shirt worn in the Revierderby in June 2020?

    A. Kinderlachen eV

    B. Save the Children

    C. Autism Bihor

    D. UNICEF

7. Which team does Haaland's maternal cousin Albert Braut Tjaaland play for?

    A. Bryne

    B. Molde

    C. Brann

    D. KFUM

8. Which of these activities is disliked by Haaland?

    A. Meditation

    B. Chopping woods

    C. Interviews

    D. Potato farming

9. How many kids does Haaland have?

    A. 3

    B. 2

    C. 1

    D. 0

10. When did Haaland's last known relationship end?

    A. 2018

    B. 2017

    C. 2019

    D. 2020

10 Trivia Answers

1. D – 20

2. A – SOS Autism Bihor

3. C – Dortmund

4. C – A referee

5. D – Dortmund

6. A – Kinderlachen eV

7. B – Molde

8. C – Interviews

9. D – 0

10. A – 2018

ERLING HAALAND CROSSWORD PUZZLE #1

ACROSS

(5) Premier League team

(6) Profession

(9) Father's name

(10) National team

DOWN

(1) Bundesliga team

(2) Where was he born?

(3) First club

(4) Premier League manager

(7) Brand deal

(8) Bundesliga manager

CHAPTER

9

PROFILE & STYLE OF PLAY

"Of course, I can't get anything over that geezer (Haaland) at the minute, I swear to God. It sums him up."

– Jude Bellingham

As a prolific goal-getter, Erling Haaland possesses all the characteristics of an all-rounded center-forward. He is 194 cm tall and uses his towering frame to hold up play and get teammates involved. He can create chances, dribble, has the pace and ability to make clever runs in behind, and can finish off chances with his head or both feet.

Sometimes, he drops deep to receive the ball as his team builds up play, then sends the ball out wide to a teammate before turning and running towards the opposition goal. At times, he drops deep so sharply that defenders cannot keep up with him, enabling him to turn on the ball and pass while facing the opposition goal.

In the penalty box, Haaland makes short, sharp runs to create an opportunity for a teammate to locate him in space, and sometimes may change the direction in which he is running, making him incredibly hard for defenders to track. He uses his sizeable frame well when playing with his back to the opposition goal, shielding the ball well as he attempts to control it, and at the same time, enabling his team's defenders to regroup after making a clearance.

Haaland's creativity is most visible when he darts into the left, from where he can either shoot or use his superb vision to spot a teammate's delayed run from deep through the middle. He also uses his pace on counterattacks to create chances for his teammates. Out of the 167 club goals Haaland has scored in his senior club career, 16 are headed goals, 22 from penalties, and the rest were scored from either foot via shots or tap-ins.

Haaland idolizes Cristiano Ronaldo and Zlatan Ibrahimović, but he has also mentioned Sergio Aguero, Robin van Persie, Jamie Vardy, and Michu as sources of inspiration. He has also acknowledged Sergio Ramos and Virgil van Dijk as two of the toughest defenders he had faced.

10 Trivia Questions

1. How tall is Erling Haaland?

    A. 190 cm

    B. 194 cm

    C. 198 cm

    D. 185 cm

2. What does Haaland use his towering frame for?

    A. Hold up play and get teammates involved

    B. Concede fouls

    C. Clear opposition attacks

    D. Knockdown opponents

3. Which of these is not among Haaland's skillset?

    A. Dribbling

    B. Creating chances

    C. Clever runs in behind

    D. Defending

4. How many headed goals has Haaland scored in his senior club career (As of February 2023)?

    A. 16

    B. 18

    C. 20

    D. 22

5. When is Haaland's creativity most visible?

    A. When he heads

    B. When he shoots

    C. When he drifts into the left flank

    D. When he scores

6. How many goals has Haaland scored from freekicks in his senior club career?

    A. 1

    B. 0

    C. 3

    D. 5

7. Which of these players is idolized by Haaland?

    A. Lionel Messi

    B. Cristiano Ronaldo

    C. Didier Drogba

    D. Raul Gonzalez

8. How many goals has Haaland scored from the penalty spot in his senior career?

    A. 31

    B. 15

    C. 13

    D. 14

9. Which of these players has been cited by Haaland as a source of inspiration?

    A. Kylian Mbappe

    B. Wayne Rooney

    C. Jamie Vardy

    D. Les Ferdinand

10. Which of these is not a good use of Haaland's sizeable frame?

    A. Hold up play

    B. Fouling opponents

    C. Scoring headers

    D. Making clearances

10 Trivia Answers

1. B – 194 cm

2. A – Hold up play and get teammates involved

3. D – Defending

4. A – 16

5. C – When he drifts into the left flank

6. B – 0

7. B – Cristiano Ronaldo

8. A – 22

9. C – Jaime Vardy

10. B – Fouling opponents

ERLING HAALAND WORD SCRAMBLE #3

1. GLISNEH IPRERME LEAEUG _____

2. SOMHPAINC GLEUEA _____

3. UFEA _____

4. SNBADILGUE _____

5. ISANRUTA GILAUNEDSB _____

6. EFLT TOFO _____

7. RFAODRW _____

8. EISRRTK _____

9. ETTACARK _____

10. DHRAEE _____

CHAPTER

10
FUTURE & LEGACY

*"I can't really predict this one. I'm told that Haaland is really
tempted to play in La Liga."*

– Fabrizio Romano

Prior to his move to Manchester City in the summer of 2022, Erling Haaland was the most sought-after striker in football. He has since built upon his reputation as a reliable goalscorer in the Northwest of England, and some still tout him as a future player of Bayern Munich or Real Madrid, whose style may fit him more than Manchester City's current possession-based style.

As one of the most talented center-forwards to grace the game of football, Haaland can shape the future generation of strikers with his exemplary traits like making short, sharp movements inside the penalty box, superb hold-up play, and near-perfect finishing.

Haaland, alongside other star players like Arsenal's Martin Odegaard, can inspire a turnaround in the fortunes of the Norwegian national team by helping to secure qualification for upcoming major tournaments like Euro 2024 and the 2026 FIFA World Cup.

Haaland has left a legacy of scoring plenty of goals at all the clubs he has played at, as well as for the Norwegian national team, for whom he has 21 goals in 23 senior caps. He scored 20 times in 50 appearances for Molde, 29 goals in 27 appearances for RB Salzburg, and 86 goals in 69 appearances for Borussia Dortmund. With still a sizeable proportion of his first season at Manchester City left, the prolific Norwegian has scored 33 goals in 33 appearances.

10 Trivia Questions

1. Where could Haaland likely move to when he decides to leave Manchester City?

    A. Manchester United

    B. Bayern Munich

    C. Al-Nassr

    D. Inter Miami

2. How many goals did Haaland score for RB Salzburg?

    A. 29

    B. 22

    C. 20

    D. 13

3. How can Haaland continue to make an impact on the Norwegian national team in the near future?

    A. By helping them to qualify for future World Cups

    B. By scoring lots of goals

    C. By helping them to qualify for future European Championships

    D. All of the above

4. How has Haaland impacted the future generation of centre-forwards?

    A. By diving

    B. By running slowly

    C. By making sharp movements in the box

    D. By doing flair tricks

5. How many goals did Haaland score for Borussia Dortmund?

    A. 70

    B. 58

    C. 86

    D. 64

6. For which of Haaland's previous clubs did he fail to score a senior goal?

    A. Bryne

    B. Molde

    C. RB Salzburg

    D. Borussia Dortmund

7. At which of these international tournaments did Haaland finish as top goalscorer?

    A. UEFA Euro 2020

    B. 2018 FIFA World Cup

    C. 2018/19 UEFA Nations League

    D. 2020/21 UEFA Nations League

8. How many World Cup matches has Haaland played (as of February 2023)?

    A. 4

    B. 2

    C. 3

    D. 0

9. Which of these is not an exemplary trait future generation of strikers can copy from Haaland?

    A. Superb hold-up play

    B. Exquisite finishing

    C. Clever runs in the box

    D. Diving

10. How many goals did Haaland score while at Molde?

    A. 10

    B. 15

    C. 20

    D. 25

10 Trivia Answers

1. B – Bayern Munich

2. A – 29

3. D – All of the above

4. C – By making sharp movements in the box

5. C – 86

6. A – Bryne

7. D – 2020/21 UEFA Nations League

8. D – 0

9. D – Diving

10. C – 20

ERLING HAALAND CROSSWORD PUZZLE #2

ACROSS

[4] Man City location

[6] Coach at RB Salzburg

[7] Number at RB Salzburg

DOWN

(1) Color of Man City jersey

(2) Number at Man City

(3) Borussia Dortmund location

(5) RB Salzburg location

(8) Color of Dortmund jersey

PUZZLE SOLUTIONS

ERLING HAALAND MAZE #1

ERLING HAALAND WORD SEARCH #1

```
M  L  B  E  R  L  I  N  G  M  R  B  D  H  B
P  T  H  H  A  A  L  A  N  D  F  K  D  U  P
B  M  D  Q  N  K  C  U  S  G  R  V  Y  C  A
I  B  Y  J  T  O  P  S  C  O  R  E  R  H  J
U  L  I  D  D  O  R  T  M  U  N  D  X  F  D
S  A  L  Z  B  U  R  G  H  N  B  G  G  C  W
E  N  G  L  A  N  D  B  C  O  U  Z  E  A  I
D  I  R  A  Z  N  S  R  W  R  N  E  R  Y  W
Z  H  C  H  U  J  I  D  H  W  D  S  M  D  L
Y  X  I  C  K  K  R  E  Q  A  E  P  A  M  Q
F  B  T  N  O  Y  M  J  O  Y  S  H  N  T  K
A  J  Y  Q  N  K  Z  B  C  S  L  M  Y  O  D
X  U  Z  C  Y  E  P  L  C  X  I  N  U  Z  X
Q  H  E  M  A  N  C  I  T  Y  G  M  Z  S  Y
E  Y  N  D  R  U  F  V  L  O  A  Z  E  Q  X
```

ERLING	EPL	DORTMUND	ENGLAND
NORWAY	BUNDESLIGA	GERMANY	MANCITY
CITYZEN	SALZBURG	HAALAND	TOPSCORER

ERLING HAALAND WORD SCRAMBLE #1

1. HCMERESTAN TYIC   MANCHESTER CITY

2. SIOSURAB UOTDDNRM   BORUSSIA DORTMUND

3. GRLINE AALNHDA   ERLING HAALAND

4. WRONAY   NORWAY

5. ELEDS   LEEDS

6. EBAUSLINGD   BUNDESLIGA

7. BR GLRSBZUA   RB SALZBURG

8. LNHISEG RPIMERE UELGEA   ENGLISH PREMIER LEAGUE

9. ERNGMAY   GERMANY

10. EPP AUIODRALG   PEP GUARDIOLA

11. NVKIE ED REUNYB   KEVIN DE BRUYNE

12. AKIYI DGGUNAON   IIKAY GUNDOGAN

13. NREBMU ENIN   NUMBER NINE

14. SOHNDMEA   HANDSOME

15. RTESKRI   STRIKER

16. LAGO RSCOER   GOAL SCORER

17. CDROER BKEARRE   RECORD BREAKER

18. FYTEL   LEFTY

19. CMAOR SREU   MARCO REUS

20. DEJU IGENHLMLAB   JUDE BELLINGHAM

ERLING HAALAND WORD SEARCH #2

```
T  G  P  B  A  E  G  I  M  I  F  H  G  Z  G
Z  H  U  N  B  C  H  E  I  G  H  T  U  Y  H
G  O  A  L  S  C  O  R  E  R  N  H  A  V  A
P  A  M  R  E  C  O  R  D  J  J  M  R  L  N
A  J  E  Q  B  B  K  T  M  F  G  A  D  S  D
C  M  W  S  X  U  O  V  M  A  R  N  I  D  S
E  N  U  M  B  E  R  N  I  N  E  C  O  B  O
Z  U  B  W  P  L  P  S  S  G  A  H  L  B  M
B  G  X  D  U  E  O  P  D  H  A  E  A  T  E
J  V  L  K  G  F  W  E  S  A  W  S  K  C  P
U  E  Y  O  A  T  E  E  U  R  R  T  W  C  A
V  Q  Z  U  A  Y  R  D  V  Q  J  E  V  F  F
Y  F  S  T  R  I  K  E  R  J  T  R  J  R  B
Z  S  K  B  P  E  Y  H  N  F  S  A  E  M  X
N  W  S  W  S  K  M  D  W  F  A  S  E  H  J
```

HANDSOME	GOALSCORER	GUARDIOLA	HEIGHT
NUMBERNINE	RECORD	SPEED	MANCHESTER
PACE	STRIKER	POWER	LEFTY

ERLING HAALAND MAZE #2

ERLING HAALAND WORD SEARCH #3

```
F  K  B  O  B  E  L  L  I  N  G  H  A  M  D
D  F  S  H  W  B  T  I  V  Y  M  R  S  Y  P
P  M  T  X  U  Q  R  R  W  K  T  B  Y  C  L
Y  E  L  L  O  W  D  L  V  T  E  E  D  P  Y
L  F  D  E  B  R  U  Y  N  E  J  W  U  S  K
B  V  P  G  U  N  D  O  G  A  N  J  V  R  B
Z  H  I  C  L  E  Z  B  S  A  N  C  H  O  A
M  O  L  D  E  T  S  R  Q  Q  G  T  B  N  S
D  Y  E  M  D  F  S  Y  Y  S  Y  W  B  Q  U
Z  I  K  A  B  R  J  N  G  O  N  C  J  O  E
U  M  M  H  L  B  S  E  A  F  R  E  U  S  S
Q  C  Q  R  E  H  V  F  G  W  A  L  K  E  R
B  A  J  E  E  X  O  K  J  D  E  F  H  M  Z
K  I  X  Z  D  L  I  G  H  T  B  L  U  E  M
X  X  B  D  S  E  B  P  K  I  A  H  H  R  S
```

GUNDOGAN	BRYNEFK	MOLDE	YELLOW
MAHREZ	BELLINGHAM	LIGHTBLUE	WALKER
SANCHO	DEBRUYNE	REUS	LEEDS

ERLING HAALAND WORD SCRAMBLE #2

1. ELINRG ___ERLING___

2. AHADNLA ___HAALAND___

3. YAONWR ___NORWAY___

4. EYBNR KF ___BRYNE FK___

5. MEDLO KF ___MOLDE FK___

6. ERD LLBU ZBLSUAGR ___RED BULL SALZBURG___

7. BIUSSOAR MDDRUNOT ___BORUSSIA DORTMUND___

8. SEMCARNTEH ICYT ___MANCHESTER CITY___

9. DEINSBAGLU ___BUNDESLIGA___

10. INEHSLG MREEPIR EUAGEL ___ENGLISH PREMIER LEAGUE___

ERLING HAALAND CROSSWORD PUZZLE #1

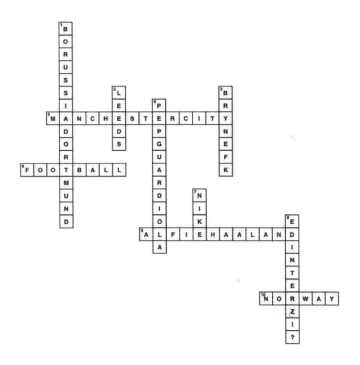

Across

[5] His Premier League team
[6] His Profession
[9] His father
[10] His National team

Down

[1] His Bundesliga team
[2] Where he was born
[3] His first club
[4] His manager in the Premier League
[7] His brand deal
[8] His Bundesliga manager

ERLING HAALAND WORD SCRAMBLE #3

1. GLISNEH IPRERME LEAEUG ___ENGLISH PREMIER LEAGUE___

2. SOMHPAINC GLEUEA ___CHAMPIONS LEAGUE___

3. UFEA ___UEFA___

4. SNBADILGUE ___BUNDESLIGA___

5. ISANRUTA GILAUNEDSB ___AUSTRIAN BUNDESLIGA___

6. EFLT TOFO ___LEFT FOOT___

7. RFAODRW ___FORWARD___

8. EISRRTK ___STRIKER___

9. ETTACARK ___ATTACKER___

10. DHRAEE ___HEADER___

ERLING HAALAND CROSSWORD PUZZLE #2

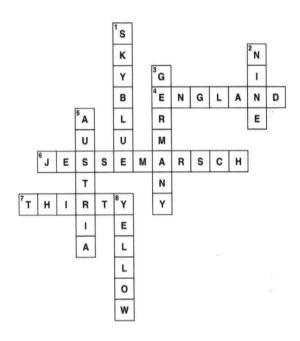

Across

[4] Where Man City is located
[6] His coach at RB Salzburg
[7] His number at RB Salzburg

Down

[1] The color of his Manchester City Jersey
[2] The number he wears at Man City
[3] Where Dortmund is located
[5] Where Salzburg is located
[8] His jersey color at Dortmund

FINAL WHISTLE

Hello, our fellow footBaller.

We really hope you enjoyed *Haaland: The Complete Story of a Football Superstar*. And congratulations on reading it to the end!

We create these books to allow football fans to expand their knowledge around their favorite clubs and players, but most importantly, to keep the passion we all have for the game lit and alive.

Life can come with many challenges and setbacks. But something that never leaves our side is our love for the game.

If you enjoyed reading this book, we'd like to kindly ask for your feedback and thoughts in the review section on Amazon.

This would really encourage us to keep creating the highest quality books and content for football fans across the globe.

>> Scan the QR Code above to leave a short review <<

Thanks in advance!

Ball out,

The House of Ballers team